FROM MY SENIOR YEARBOOK

Annette LaPlaca, *editor*

Harold Shaw Publishers
Wheaton, Illinois

Copyright © 1992 by Harold Shaw Publishers

Editor: Annette LaPlaca

Cover, design, & illustrations © 1992 by Turnbaugh & Associates

ISBN 0-87788-398-X

Library of Congress Cataloging-in-Publication Data

It came from my senior yearbook : pocket guide to Life 101 / Annette LaPlaca, editor.

   p. cm.

  Includes bibliographical references.

  ISBN 0-87788-398-X

  1. Conduct of life—Quotations, maxims, etc. I. LaPlaca, Annette Heinrich, 1964-

PN6084.C556I85 1992

082—dc20

                                            91-41801

                                              CIP

                                              AC

99 98 97 96 95 94 93 92

10 9 8 7 6 5 4 3 2

CONTENTS

Congratulations! *1*

Changing Directions *9*

Making Decisions *13*

Keeping the Faith *19*

Living in the Light *24*

Putting Something In *31*

Staying on the Bright Side *40*

Growing Friendships *50*

Looking for Love *58*

Building Character *64*

Great Expectations *74*

Index *83*

CONGRATULATIONS!

Congratulations! Give yourself a pat on the
back—graduation is an achievement to be proud of.
Take time to enjoy the sweet taste of success.

Graduation is a ceremony that marks the end of study and
the beginning of education. *Evan Esar,* Esar's Comic
Dictionary

■

We do not know who we are until we see what we can do.
Martha Grimes, Writer's Handbook, *in* Reader's Digest

■

No man ever reached to excellence in any one art or
profession without having passed through the slow and
painful process of study and preparation. *Horace*

■

Education is discipline for the adventure of life. *Alfred
North Whitehead*

■

The test of a truly educated man is what he is, and what
he thinks, and what his mind absorbs, or dreams, or
creates, when he is alone. *Donald K. David*

■

The object of education is to prepare the young to educate
themselves throughout their lives. *Robert Hutchins*

1

Love of learning is seldom unrequited. *Arnold H. Glasow*

∎

Education is the ability to listen to almost anything without losing your temper or your self-confidence. *Robert Frost*

∎

Genius is one per cent inspiration, and ninety-nine per cent perspiration. *Thomas Edison*

∎

Education is proceeding from cocksure ignorance to thoughtful uncertainty. *Kenneth Johnson*

∎

Human knowledge is an island in a vast sea of the unknown. *Sir Isaac Newton*

∎

Education is a companion which no misfortune can decrease, no crime destroy, no enemy alienate, no despotism enslave; at home a friend, abroad an introduction, in solitude a solace, in society an ornament. *Jo Petty,* Apples of Gold

∎

Man's reach is always greater than his grasp, his achievements never equal his aspiration, his successes never equal his attempts, his answers never equal his questions. Such is life. *Dan C. Shannon*

2

■

Success is faithfulness. . . . Success, then, comes when we faithfully study God's Word and faithfully obey it, applying what we understand to all areas of our lives under the direction of the Holy Spirit.   *Kent and Barbara Hughes,* Liberating Ministry

■

We must continually use the measure of our obedience to the guidelines of His Word as the real—and only—standard of our "success," not some more supposedly tangible or glamorous scale.   *Charles Colson,* Who Speaks for God?

■

Knowledge puffs up, but love builds up. The man who thinks he knows something does not yet know as he ought to know. But the man who loves God is known by God. *1 Corinthians 8:1-3*

■

I couldn't wait for success. . . . So I went ahead without it. *Jonathan Winters*

■

He who merits praise he never receives is better off than he who receives praise he never merits.   *Keith L. Brooks,* The Cream Book: Sentence Sermons

■

The educated man is one who has finally discovered that there are some questions to which nobody has answers. *Unknown*

3

■

Every man has two educations—that which is given to him, and the other, that which he gives to himself. Of the two kinds, the latter is by far the more valuable. Indeed, all that is most worthy in a man, he must work out and conquer for himself. *Jean Paul Richter*

■

Education is an admirable thing, but it is well to remember from time to time that nothing that is worth knowing can be taught. *Oscar Wilde*

■

Perfect wisdom has four parts: wisdom, the principle of doing things right; justice, the principle of doing things equally in public and private; fortitude, the principle of not fleeing danger, but meeting it; and temperance, the principle of subduing desires, and living moderately. *Plato*

■

If you have knowledge, let others light their candles by it. *Thomas Fuller*

■

If a man be enducd with a generous mind, this is the best kind of nobility. *Seneca*

■

It is not what we read, but what we remember, that makes us learned. It is not what we intend, but what we do, that makes us useful. It is not a few faint wishes, but a lifelong struggle, that makes us valiant. *Henry Ward Beecher*

■

The worst use that can be made of success is to boast of it.
Arthur Helps

■

It isn't what you know but what you are willing to learn.
Cliff Schimmels, T-shirt Wisdom for the Graduate

■

I am sufficiently proud of my knowing something to be
modest about my not knowing everything.   *Vladimir
Nabokov*

5

■

A man who is truly great doesn't have to prove it; and if he isn't great, trying to prove it will do no good. *Robert C. Savage,* Pocket Quips

■

The greatest ignorance is being proud of learning. *Unknown*

■

But as for you, continue in what you have learned and become convinced of, because you know those from whom you learned it, and how from infancy you have known the holy Scriptures, which are able to make you wise for salvation through faith in Christ Jesus. All Scripture is God-breathed and is useful for teaching, rebuking, correcting and training in righteousness, so that the man of God may be thoroughly equipped for every good work. *2 Timothy 3:14-17*

■

Education is the knowledge of how to use the whole of oneself. . . . A man is educated who knows how to make a tool of every faculty—how to open it, how to keep it sharp, and how to apply it to all practical purposes. *Henry Ward Beecher*

■

The secret of success is a secret to many people. *Evan Esar,* Esar's Comic Dictionary

It is the work that God does through us that counts, not what we do for Him. All that our Lord heeds in a man's life is the relationship of worth to his Father. *Oswald Chambers*, My Utmost for His Highest

Next in importance to freedom and justice is education, without which neither freedom nor justice can be permanently maintained. *James A. Garfield*

He who has no inclination to learn more will be very apt to think that he knows enough. *A. Powell*

Knowledge humbleth the great man, astonishes the common man, puffeth up the little man. *Keith L. Brooks*, The Cream Book: Sentence Sermons

In the Christian life there are many promotions in spiritual growth, but there is no graduation. *T.J. Bach*

Knowledge comes but wisdom lingers. *Alfred Lord Tennyson*

Real success is more of an inward feeling than an outward show. *Unknown*

■

Thought and learning are of small value unless translated into action. *Wang Ming*

■

If at first you don't succeed, you have plenty of company.
Eldon Pedersen

■

Without experience one gains no wisdom. *Chinese proverb*

■

Success comes from wide-awake days rather than sleepless nights. *Unknown*

■

It is nonsense to talk of the college years as only a preparation for life. They are part of life. *Paul Swain Havens*

■

Wisdom is the scar tissue of intelligence. *Gene Gleason*

■ ■ ■ ■ ■ ■ ■ ■ ■ ■ ■ ■ ■ ■ ■ ■ ■

CHANGING DIRECTIONS

Graduation is a crossroads place in life.
From here you'll go on to new challenges, new experiences.
Exciting changes lie ahead!

"Forget the former things;
do not dwell on the past.
See, I am doing a new thing!" *Isaiah 43:18-19*

■

Two roads diverged in a wood, and I—
I took the one less traveled by,
And that has made all the difference.
Robert Frost, "The Road Not Taken"

■

"I am the way and the truth and the life. No one comes to
the Father except through me." *Jesus Christ, John 14:6*

■

Change, like sunshine, can be a friend or a foe, a blessing
or a curse, a dawn or a dusk. *William Arthur Ward*

■

It will do no good to get on the right track if you then go
in the wrong direction. *Evan Esar,* Esar's Comic Dictionary

■

Change is the law of life and growth. *C.B. Eavey,* 2500
Sentence Sermons

9

■

Stand at the crossroads and look; ask for the ancient
paths, ask where the good way is, and walk in it, and you
will find rest for your souls. *Jeremiah 6:16*

■

Change is the only constant thing in the universe. *Unknown*

■

Education consists of knowing where to get knowledge
when you need it, and then how to organize that knowledge into definite plans of action. *Napoleon Hill*

■

We live in a crazy world and the only way to see it is to
stand permanently on your head. *G.K. Chesterton*

■

Spring is a promise
in the closed fist
of a long winter
Luci Shaw, "Faith," Postcard from the Shore

■

You have made known to me the path of life;
you will fill me with joy in your presence,
with eternal pleasures at your right hand.
Psalm 16:11

■

The Father comes near to take our hand and lead us on
our way. *Mrs. Charles E. Cowman,* Streams in the Desert

Jesus tells us that there can be no religion without adventure, and that God can find no use for the shut mind.
William Barclay, The Gospel of Matthew, *on the parable of the talents*

∎

The only way to get anywhere is to start from where you are. *William Lee*

∎

Dare to trust Him; dare to follow Him! *F.B. Meyer*

∎

WAIT

These are
the good
old days.
Just wait
and see.
Steve Turner, Up-to-Date

∎

No man can follow Christ and go astray. *Faunce*

∎

There is a kind of happiness and wonder that makes you serious. *C.S. Lewis,* The Last Battle

∎

A good beginning is likely to mean a good ending.
Unknown

■

Lord, the newness of this day
Calls me to an untried way:
Let me gladly take the road,
Give me strength to bear my load,
Thou my guide and helper be—
I will travel through with Thee. *Henry van Dyke*

■

How often we look upon God as our last and feeblest resource! We go to Him because we have nowhere else to go. And then we learn that the storms of life have driven us, not upon the rocks, but into the desired haven. *George MacDonald*

■

Even if you're on the right track, you'll be run over if you sit still. *Unknown*

■

Ideals are like stars. You will never succeed in touching them with your hands; but, like the seafaring man on the desert of waters, you choose them as your guide, and following them, reach your destination. *Carl Schurz*

■

Don't think you are necessarily on the right road just because it is a well-beaten path. *Unknown*

■ ■ ■ ■ ■ ■ ■ ■ ■ ■ ■ ■ ■ ■ ■ ■ ■

MAKING DECISIONS

Part of moving out in new directions is making decisions about
things like career and relationships. Your day-to-day
choices in these big questions will shape much of your life.

Choices are the hinges of destiny. *Edwin Markham*

■

Trust in the LORD with all your heart
and lean not on your own understanding;
in all your ways acknowledge him,
and he will make your paths straight.
Proverbs 3:5-6

■

What would Jesus do? *Charles Sheldon,* In His Steps

■

O Thou, who are the God no less of those who know thee
not than of those who know thee well, be present with us
at the times of choosing when time stands still and all that
lies behind and all that lies ahead are caught up in the
mystery of a moment. *Frederick Buechner,* The Hungering Dark

■

Destiny is not a matter of chance, it is a matter of choice.
Unknown

13

■

Whether you turn to the right or to the left, your ears will hear a voice behind you, saying, "This is the way, walk in it." *Isaiah 30:21*

■

Every day we choose good or evil, right or wrong, holiness or sin, God or Satan. *C.B. Eavey,* 2500 Sentence Sermons

■

Great minds have purposes; others have wishes.
Washington Irving

■

A decision is what a person makes when he can't get anyone to serve on a committee. *Fletcher Knebel*

■

He who deliberates fully before taking a step will spend his entire life on one leg. *Chinese proverb*

■

Not to decide is to decide. *Unknown*

■

Commit to the LORD whatever you do,
and your plans will succeed.
Proverbs 16:3

■

I thought
I was losing
my mind.

It was only
my imagination.
David Porter, "Suburbia Poem"

■

The greatest mistake you can make is to be continually
fearing that you'll make one. *Elbert Hubbard*

■

For you as a Christian, guidance is meant to be an aspect
of your ongoing relationship with God. He wants you to
know him. Being guided by him is part of that. *John
White*, The Fight

■

The strongest pain of growth lies in human choice.
George Eliot

■

A little uncertainty is good for everyone. *Henry Kissinger*

■

Patience is what you have when you don't know what to
do next. *Unknown*

■

Nothing is so exhausting as indecision, and nothing is so
futile. *Bertrand Russell*

■

Be transformed by the renewing of your mind. Then you
will be able to test and approve what God's will is—his
good, pleasing and perfect will. *Romans 12:2-3*

■

In all decisions, the believer should humbly submit, in
advance, to the outworking of God's sovereign will as it
touches each decision.   *Garry Friesen,* Decision-Making and the
Will of God

■

I will instruct you and teach you in the way you should
go.   *Psalm 32:8*

■

To every man there openeth
A High Way, and a Low.
And every man decideth
The way his soul should go.   *John Oxenham*

■

If we are ever in doubt what to do, it is a good rule to ask
ourselves what we shall wish on the morrow that we had
done.   *Lord Avebury*

■

Living is a form of not being sure, not knowing what next
or how. . . . We may be wrong, but we take leap after leap
in the dark.   *Agnes De Mille*

■

Free will is not the liberty to do whatever one likes, but
the power of doing whatever one sees ought to be done,
even in the very face of otherwise overwhelming impulse.
There lies freedom, indeed.   *George MacDonald*

■

We know what happens to people who stay in the middle of the road. They get run over. *Aneurin Bevan*

■

I don't know the key to success, but the key to failure is trying to please everybody. *Bill Cosby*

■

God asks no man whether he will accept life. That is not the choice. You must take it. The only choice is how. *Henry Ward Beecher*

17

■

It does not take much strength to do things, but it requires great strength to decide on what to do. *Elbert Hubbard*

■

It is not in life's chances but in life's choices that happiness comes to the heart of the individual. *C.B. Eavey,* 2500 Sentence Sermons

■

Take courage when you have a tough decision to make. Someone who cares deeply for you already knows what he wants you do do. He takes delight in having fellowship with you and wants the very circumstances you face to draw you closer to him. *John White,* The Fight

■

Let me be acutely attuned to Your Word, so that each decision I have to make will be in Your will, almighty God. *Billy Graham,* Day by Day

■

Once to every man and nation comes the moment to
    decide,
In the strife of Truth and Falsehood, for the good or evil
    side. *J.R. Lowell*

■ ■ ■ ■ ■ ■ ■ ■ ■ ■ ■ ■ ■ ■ ■ ■

KEEPING THE FAITH

Your acceptance of salvation and trust in the Lord
form a foundation of faith. Build confidently
on this foundation—God keeps his promises (see Matthew 7:24).

I believe in Christianity as I believe the sun has risen, not
only because I see it but because by it I see everything
else. *C.S. Lewis*

Faith means believing what is incredible, or it is no virtue
at all. Hope means hoping when things are hopeless, or it
is no virtue at all. And charity means pardoning what is
unpardonable, or it is no virtue at all. *G.K. Chesterton,*
Heretics

Faith is to believe what we do not see. The reward of this
faith is to see what we believe. *St. Augustine*

Faith is being sure of what we hope for and certain of
what we do not see. *Hebrews 11:1*

Faith is not contrary to reason, but rather "reason grown
courageous." *Sherwood Eddy*

Faith is saying "Amen" to God. *Merv Rosell*

■

Doubt isn't the opposite of faith; it is an element of faith.
Paul Tillich

■

Faith is the confidence that God's Word is true and the
conviction that acting upon that Word will bring his blessing. *Robert C. Savage,* Pocket Quips

■

Faith expects from God what is beyond expectation.
Unknown

■

Faith is necessary in *everything*. *J.B. Stoney*

■

Faith is dependence on God. And this God-dependence
only begins when self-dependence ends. *James McConkey*

■

The highest pinnacle of the spiritual life is not joy in un-
broken sunshine but absolute and undoubting trust in the
love of God. *A.W. Thorold*

■

Faith is being able to see with your heart what you cannot
see with your eyes. *Robert C. Savage,* Pocket Quips

■

The beginning of anxiety is the end of faith, and the
beginning of true faith is the end of anxiety. *George
Müller*

■

Faith, walking in the dark with God, only prays Him to
clasp its hand more closely.   *Phillips Brooks*

■

We have no more faith at any time than we have in the
hour of trial. . . . Fair-weather faith is no faith.   *Charles H.
Spurgeon*

■

"In repentance and rest is your salvation,
in quietness and trust is your strength."   *Isaiah 30:15*

■

Faith is at the core of practical Christianity. Your Christian life began when you began to believe. It has grown
and will grow as faith widens the channel along which
grace flows to you. No aspect of your Christian life is of
greater importance.   *John White,* The Fight

■

God delights to increase the faith of His Children.   *George
Müller*

■

Faith adds surety to the expectation of hope.   *Jo Petty,*
Apples of Gold

■

Never try to arouse faith from within. You cannot stir up
faith from the depths of your heart. Leave your heart, and
look into the face of Christ.   *Andrew Murray*

21

•

Doubt sees the obstacles; Faith sees the way. *Robert C. Savage,* Pocket Quips

•

Faith comes from hearing the message, and the message is heard through the word of Christ. *Romans 10:17*

•

Faith is just believing what God says he will do.
He will never fail us; His promises are true.
If we but believe Him, His children we become.
Faith is just believing this wondrous thing is done.
Children's song

•

It is not the greatness of my faith that moves mountains, but my faith in the greatness of God. *Unknown*

•

Nothing is impossible to men of faith and conviction.
T.S. Eliot

•

When you get all wrinkled with care and worry, it's time for a *faith* lift. *C.B. Eavey,* 2500 Sentence Sermons

•

Without faith it is impossible to please God, because anyone who comes to him must believe that he exists and that he rewards those who earnestly seek him. *Hebrews 11:6*

■

Tis so sweet to trust in Jesus,
ust to take Him at His word,
ust to rest upon His promise,
ust to know, "Thus saith the Lord."
Louisa M.R. Stead, "Tis So Sweet to Trust in Jesus"

■

Faith is not some kind of nebulous feeling that we work
up. Faith is confidence that God's Word is true, and the
conviction that acting upon that Word will bring his blessing. *Robert C. Savage,* Pocket Quips

■

Faith is man's response to God's initiative. *John White,*
The Fight

■

Faith by itself, if it is not accompanied by action, is
dead. . . . Show me your faith without deeds, and I will
show you my faith by what I do. *James 2:17-18*

■

If the Sun and Moon should doubt,
They'd immediately go out.
William Blake

■

Faith is the soul's venture; it ventures all on Christ. *Unknown*

■ ■ ■ ■ ■ ■ ■ ■ ■ ■ ■ ■ ■ ■ ■

23

LIVING IN THE LIGHT

In this fast-paced, multi-media, hyper-active world,
make it your number-one goal to love and serve your Savior.
Seeking the abundant life Jesus promised means
keeping in step with the Spirit (see John 10:10; Galatians 5:25).

Being confident of this, that he who began a good work in
you will carry it on to completion until the day of Christ
Jesus. *Philippians 1:6*

■

May I run the race before me,
Strong and brave to face the foe,
Looking only unto Jesus
As I onward go.
Kate B. Wilkinson, "May the Mind of Christ My Savior"

■

Whatsoever weakens your reason, impairs the tenderness
of your conscience, obscures your sense of God, or takes
off the relish of spiritual things—whatsoever increases the
authority of your body over your mind—that thing, to
you, is sin. *Susanna Wesley*

■

Do you not know that in a race all the runners run, but
only one gets the prize? Run in such a way as to get the
prize. *1 Corinthians 9:24*

24

■

The soul that has once been waked, or stung, or uplifted by the desire of God, will inevitably (I think) awake to the fear of losing Him. *C.S. Lewis,* Letters to Malcolm

■

I had far rather walk, as I do, in daily terror of eternity, than feel that this was only a children's game in which all the contestants would get equally worthless prizes in the end. *T.S. Eliot*

■

If our circumstances find us in God, we shall find God in our circumstances. *George Müller*

■

For our light and momentary troubles are achieving for us an eternal glory that far outweighs them all. So we fix our eyes not on what is seen, but on what is unseen. For what is seen is temporary, but what is unseen is eternal. *2 Corinthians 4:17-18*

■

The grand essentials to happiness in this life are something to do, something to love, and something to hope for. *Joseph Addison*

■

The life of a man is a thing of potential beauty and dignity. . . . To live is good. *Unknown*

■

Life oughta come with directions! *Jeff and Ramona Tucker*

■

One can never consent to creep when one feels an impulse to soar. *Helen Keller*

■

True religion is the life we live, not the creed we profess. *J.F. Wright*

Dost thou love life? Then waste not time; for time is the stuff that life is made of. *Benjamin Franklin*

■

Life is no brief candle to me. It is a sort of splendid torch which I am permitted to hold for the moment, and I want to make it burn as brightly as possible before handing it on to future generations. *George Bernard Shaw*

■

Sooner or later a man, if he is wise, discovers that life is a mixture of good days and bad, victory and defeat, give and take. *Unknown*

■

We make a living by what we get, but we make a life by what we give. *Herbert V. Prochnow*

■

It takes the whole of life to learn how to live. *Jo Petty,* Apples of Gold

■

Jesus said to her, "I am the resurrection and the life. He who believes in me will live, even though he dies; and whoever lives and believes in me will never die." *John 11:25-26*

■

A mighty fortress is our God,
A bulwark never failing.

Our helper, he, amid the flood
of mortal ills prevailing.
Martin Luther

■

Courage is grace under pressure.   *Ernest Hemingway*

■

We should concentrate on living within today. Then better
tomorrows will inevitably follow.   *Dale Carnegie*

■

And the days are not full enough
And the nights are not full enough
And life slips by like a field mouse
Not shaking the grass.
Ezra Pound

■

Life—a little gleam of time between two eternities.
Thomas Carlyle

■

God's in his heaven—all's right with the world!   *Robert
Browning*

■

Give your life to God; He can do more with it than you
can!   *Dwight L. Moody*

■

Command those who are rich in this present world not to
be arrogant nor to put their hope in wealth, which is so

uncertain, but to put their hope in God, who richly provides us with everything for our enjoyment. Command them to do good, to be rich in good deeds, and to be generous and willing to share. In this way they will lay up treasure for themselves as a firm foundation for the coming age, so that they may take hold of the life that is truly life. *1 Timothy 6:17-19*

■

The Bible is God's road map. *Kenyon Palmer*

■

God is always whispering to us, only we do not hear, because of the noise, hurry, and distraction which life causes as it rushes on. *F.W. Faber*

■

The Christian ideal has not been tried and found wanting, it has been found difficult and left untried. *G.K. Chesterton*

■

One can never pay in gratitude; one can only pay "in kind" somewhere else in life. *Anne Morrow Lindbergh*

■

One of the great arts of living is the art of forgetting. *Unknown*

■

The real art of living is beginning where you are. *Unknown*

■

To be patient in little things, to be tolerant in large affairs, to be happy in the midst of petty cares and monotonies, that is wisdom. *Joseph Fort Newton*

■

Blessed is the man who has found his work. *Elbert Hubbard*

■

To laugh often and love much

To win the respect of intelligent persons and the affection of children

To earn the approbation of honest critics and endure the betrayal of false friends

To appreciate beauty

To find the best in others

To give one's self

To leave the world a bit better, whether by a healthy child, a garden patch or a redeemed social condition

To have played and laughed with enthusiasm and sung with exultation

To know even one life has breathed easier because you have lived—

This is to have succeeded. *Ralph Waldo Emerson*

■

Each new day is an opportunity to start all over again . . . to cleanse our minds and hearts anew and to clarify our vision. *Jo Petty,* Apples of Gold

■ ■ ■ ■ ■ ■ ■ ■ ■ ■ ■ ■ ■ ■ ■ ■ ■

PUTTING SOMETHING IN

It's easy to sit back and enjoy the blessings of life,
but it's exciting to get out there and put something
excellent, worthwhile, and true into the wide
world—something unique only you can contribute.

That best portion of a good man's life—his little, name-
less, unremembered acts of kindness and of love. *William
Wordsworth*

■

Seek always to do good somewhere. You must give some
time to your fellow man. For remember, you don't live in
a world all your own. *Albert Schweitzer*

■

Expect great things from God. Attempt great things for
God. *William Carey*

■

The world is before you, and you need not take it or leave
it as it was when you came in. *James Baldwin*

■

Service is love in working clothes. *Keith L. Brooks,* The
Cream Book: Sentence Sermons

■

Never put off till tomorrow what you can do today.
Thomas Jefferson, Ben Franklin

31

PUT SOMETHING IN

Draw a crazy picture
Write a nutty poem,
Sing a mumble-gumble song,
Whistle through your comb.
Do a loony-goony dance,
'Cross the kitchen floor,
Put something silly in the world
That ain't been there before.

Shel Silverstein, A Light in the Attic

Awake, arise, or be forever fallen! *John Milton*

■

Life is like a game of tennis. The player who serves well
seldom loses! *Robert C. Savage,* Pocket Quips

■

Our will, done in our own strength, is humanism. Christ's
will, done in our own strength, is religion. And his will,
done by his power, is the abundant life. *Lloyd John Ogilvie*

■

The vocation of every man and woman is to serve other
people. *Unknown*

■

Small deeds done are better than great deeds planned.
Peter Marshall

■

To accomplish great things, we must not only act but also
dream, not only plan but also believe. *Anatole France*

■

The man who removes a mountain begins by carrying
away small stones. *Chinese proverb*

■

The world is moved not only by the mighty shoves of the
heroes but also by the aggregate of the tiny pushes of each
honest worker. *Helen Keller*

■

It is only when we forget ourselves that we do things that are remembered. *Unknown*

■

A man's true wealth is the good he does in this world.
Mohammed

■

"Who is a wise man and endued with knowledge among you? Let him shew out of a good conversation his works with meekness of wisdom" *James 3:13, KJV*

■

With this kind of wisdom and knowledge, we may enter upon our chosen field of service and there find satisfaction and blessing, together with the tranquility of one who is subordinated to the yoke of Jesus Christ. *Hudson T. Armerding,* A Word to the Wise

■

A Christian man is the most free lord of all, and subject to none; a Christian man is the most dutiful servant of all, and subject to everyone. *Martin Luther*

■

Wherever there is a human being, there is an opportunity for kindness. *Seneca*

■

Trust in God and *do* something. *Mary Lyon*

Lost time is never found again. *Benjamin Franklin*

The smallest good deed is better than the grandest intention. *Unknown*

Not unless we fill our existence with an aim do we make it life. *Reichel*

Our heavenly Father never gives us too much to do. . . . He knows what He wants from each of us, and there is plenty of time in His day for things essential to His plan. *Charles Shedd,* Time for All Things

A man can do only what he can do. But if he does that each day, he can sleep at night and do it again the next day. *Albert Schweitzer*

There never was a bad man but had ability for good service. *Edmund Burke*

The best place to find a helping hand is at the end of your arm. *Elmer Leterman*

They who have learned the way to live,
    Plant wisely, though they may not reap;

And this is well, since what we give
  Is all that we may hope to keep.
Margaret E. Bruner

I love the word impossible. *Ann Kiemel*

Too low they build who build beneath the stars. *Unknown*

The only gift is a portion of thyself. *Ralph Waldo Emerson*

If good and godly men stand aloof from moral and
societal obligations in matters civic or spiritual, social or
educational, their dereliction of duty creates a vacuum to

e filled by the ambitious and unprincipled. *V. Raymond Edman*, Great Sermons of the Twentieth Century

■

Once we see the world and ourselves for what we are, we can help. Once we understand ourselves we begin to operate not from a posture of anger but of compassion and concern. We look at the world not with bitter frowns but with extended hands. We realize that the lights are out and a lot of people are stumbling in the darkness. So we light candles. *Max Lucado*, No Wonder They Call Him the Savior

■

Do good with what thou hast, or it will do thee no good. *William Penn*

■

Holiness is religious principle put into action. . . . It is faith gone to work. It is love coined into conduct; devotion helping human suffering, and going up in intercession to the great source of all good. *F.D. Huntington*

■

We never know how high we are
Till we are called to rise;
And then, if we are true to plan,
Our statures touch the skies.
Emily Dickinson

■

It is better to busy oneself about the smallest thing in the world than to treat a half-hour as worthless. *Goethe*

37

Give what you have. To some one it may be better than you dare to think. *Henry Wadsworth Longfellow*

■

Never be lacking in zeal, but keep your spiritual fervor, serving the Lord. *Romans 12:11*

■

We cannot do everything at once, but we can do something at once. *Calvin Coolidge*

■

Far and away the best prize that life offers is the chance to work hard at work worth doing. *Theodore Roosevelt*

■

That which we persist in doing becomes easier for us to do, not that the nature of the thing itself is changed, but that our power to do is increased. *Ralph Waldo Emerson*

■

It is possible to be so active in the service of Christ as to forget to love him. . . . Christ can do without your works; what he wants is you. Yet if he really has you, he will have all your works. *P.T. Forsyth*

■

Action springs not from thought, but from a readiness for responsibility. *Dietrich Bonhoeffer,* Letters and Papers from Prison

■

Individuality is the salt of common life. . . . Be yourself if you would serve others. *Henry Van Dyke*

■

I shall pass this way but once; if, therefore, there be any kindness I can show, or any good thing I can do to my fellow human beings, let me do it now; let me not defer nor neglect it, for I shall pass this way but once. *Abraham Lincoln*

■ ■ ■ ■ ■ ■ ■ ■ ■ ■ ■ ■ ■ ■ ■

STAYING ON THE BRIGHT SIDE

Life gets stressful; pressures of all kinds can stretch you to your very limits. During times like those, it's important to invest some time in laughter. Seek the joy of the Lord, and the "bright side" of your circumstances will eventually appear.

Laff every time you pheel tickled, and laff once in a while enyhow. *Josh Billings*

Laughter is the shortest distance between two people.
Victor Borge

Humor is emotional chaos remembered in tranquility.
James Thurber

Wit has truth in it; wisecracking is simply calisthenics with words. *Dorothy Parker*

A little nonsense now and then
Is relished by the wisest men.
Anonymous

Laughter is the sensation of feeling good all over, and showing it principally in one spot. *Josh Billings*

Laugh and the world laughs with you,
Weep and you weep alone,
For the sad old earth must borrow its mirth,
But has trouble enough of its own.
Ella Wheeler Wilcox

■

He who laughs, lasts.   *Mary Pettibone Poole*

■

I am never more tickled than when I laugh at myself.
Mark Twain

■

Laughter is the music of the soul.   *C.B. Eavey*, 2500 Sentence
Sermons

■

Let a smile be your umbrella—and you'll get a mouthful
of rain!   *Unknown*

■

■

Let us be determined to be happy; make the most of the
blessings that come to us; look on the bright side of everything. Cheerfulness is not always spontaneous. . . . One
who can carry a smiling face through a world where there
are so many troubled hearts may unconsciously be a

public benefactor; for "the merry heart doeth good like a medicine," and not alone to its possessor.   *M.P. Wells*

■

Enjoy yourself. It is later than you think.   *Chinese proverb*

■

He is not laughed at that laughs at himself first.   *Thomas Fuller*

■

It is a poor heart that never rejoices.   *Anne Fremantle*

■

Those who do not know how to weep do not know how to laugh either.   *Golda Meir*

■

Humor lightens human burdens.   *Grenville Kleiser*

■

The cheerful heart has a continual feast.   *Proverbs 15:15*

■

Grief melts away
Like snow in May,
As if there were no such cold thing.
George Herbert, "The Flower"

■

A smile is the lighting system of the face and the heating system of the heart.   *Robert C. Savage,* Pocket Quips

42

■

Happiness is like a pair of eyeglasses correcting your spiritual vision.   *Lloyd Morris*

■

The surest way to be miserable is to have the leisure to wonder whether or not you are happy.   *George Bernard Shaw*

■

Happiness is a warm puppy.   *Charles Schultz*

■

If you "keep smiling," people will wonder what you've been up to.   *Unknown*

■

The world is like a mirror, reflecting what you do; and if your face is smiling, it smiles right back at you.   *Unknown*

■

Laughter is real medicine. It has optimistic vitamins in it. It revives like oxygen. It restores failing morale. I have proved for myself the "cleansing power of laughter."
Gelett Burgess, "On Laughter"

■

Laughter is the best medicine.   *Readers Digest*

■

A cheerful heart is good medicine.   *Proverbs 17:22*

■

Life is short, and we never have too much time for gladdening the hearts of those who are traveling the dark way with us. Oh, be swift to love! Make haste to be kind!
Henri Amiel

■

Most folks are about as happy as they make up their minds to be. *Abraham Lincoln*

■

God weeps with us so that we may one day laugh with him. *Jurgen Mottmann*

■

No one is exempt from talking nonsense; the mistake is to do it solemnly. *Michael Montaigne*

■

HAPPY THOUGHT

The world is so full of a number of things,
I'm sure we should all be as happy as kings.
Robert Louis Stevenson

■

It is enough that you and I,
    Whatever be our girth,
Shake a fist at fret and gloom,
    And gird the day with mirth.
Father Jerome

The happiness in your life depends on the character of your thoughts. *Marcus Aurelius*

Finally, brothers, whatever is true, whatever is noble, whatever is right, whatever is pure, whatever is lovely, whatever is admirable—if anything is excellent or praiseworthy—think about such things. *Philippians 4:8*

'Tis easy enough to be pleasant,
When life flows along like a song;
But the man worth while is the one who will smile
When everything goes dead wrong.
Ella Wheeler Wilcox

Much may be known of a man by what excites his laughter. *Goethe*

All people smile in the same language. *Unknown*

Happiness is a thing to be practiced—like a violin. *Unknown*

ETERNITY

He who binds to himself a joy
Does the winged life destroy;

But he who kisses the joy as it flies
Lives in eternity's sun rise.   *William Blake*

■

If you can't crown yourself with laurels, you can at least
wreathe your face in smiles.   *Unknown*

■

A laugh can be a powerful thing.   *Roger Rabbit*

■

Smile, once in a while,
   'Twill make your heart seem lighter.
Smile, once in a while,
   'Twill make your pathway brighter.

Life's a mirror, if we smile
  Smiles come back to greet us;
If we're frowning all the while
  Frowns for ever meet us.   *Nixon Waterman*

■

Satisfy us in the morning with your unfailing love,
that we may sing for joy and be glad all our days.   *Psalm
90:14*

■

A warm smile thaws the icy stare.   *Merv Rosell*

■

If you would find greater joy in life, attempt to serve and
please someone every day. The gift of yourself to someone who needs you will, in return, bring the gift of confidence and serenity to you.   *John H. Crowe*

■

Every cloud has a silver lining.   *Unknown*

■

Be happy, young man, while you are young,
and let your heart give you joy in the days of your youth.
Ecclesiastes 11:9

■

They might not need me—yet they might—
I'll let my heart be just in sight—
A smile so small as mine might be
Precisely their necessity.   *Emily Dickinson*

■

True humor springs not more from the head than from the heart; it is not contempt, its essence is love; it issues not in laughter, but in smiles, which lie far deeper. *Thomas Carlyle*

■

I'm a cheerful sort of man and very disposed to laughter. You wouldn't believe . . . the number of things that strike me as being funny. I can laugh at pretty nearly everything, I can. *Uncle Albert Wigg, in* Mary Poppins, *P.L. Travers*

■

There is no duty we underrate so much as the duty of being happy. *Robert Louis Stevenson*

■

You grow up the day you have your first real laugh—at yourself. *Unknown*

■

Grin and bear it. *Unknown*

■

It is better in the long run to possess an absess or a tumor
Than to possess a sense of humor.
People who have senses of humor have a very good time,
But they never accomplish anything of note, either
   despicable or sublime,
Because how can anybody accomplish anything immortal
When they realize they look pretty funny doing it and
   have to stop to chortle.
Ogden Nash, "Don't Grin, or You'll Have to Bear It"

■

What indescribable joy!—joy over God the Almighty. . . .
For this is the absolute joy, to adore the almighty power
with which God the Almighty bears all thy care and sorrow as easily as nothing.   *Vernard Eller*

■

LESSON FROM A SUNDIAL

Ignore dull days; forget the showers;
Keep count of only shining hours.
Found on a sundial in Germany

■

Give me a smile—that flash of hidden gold
   Within the heart,
That hint of harmony and good untold,
   Of which—we all are a part!
A smile—born of a cheerful thought,
   A word of hope, a jest;
Is a thing by angels wrought,
   'Tis love—made manifest!   *Unknown*

■

It must be said that we can have joy, and therefore will
have it, only as we give it to others.   *Karl Barth*

■

I wish you all the joy you can wish.   *William Shakespeare*

■ ■ ■ ■ ■ ■ ■ ■ ■ ■ ■ ■ ■ ■ ■ ■ ■

GROWING FRIENDSHIPS

Office deadlines, career challenges, favorite hobbies—when
all these things are gone we'll see that only people
last forever. Your investment of yourself in the lives of
other people is treasure laid up in heaven (see Matthew 6:20-21).

Friendship is like money, easier made than kept. *Samuel Butler*

Our human relationships are the actual conditions in
which the ideal life of God is to be exhibited. *Oswald Chambers,* My Utmost for His Highest

A friend is a person who goes around saying nice things
about you behind your back. *Unknown*

Sympathy is two hearts tugging at the same load. *Carl S. Winters*

We are born helpless. As soon as we are fully conscious,
we discover loneliness. We need others physically, emo-
tionally, intellectually; we need them if we are to know
anything, even ourselves. *C.S. Lewis*

■

We stand in the light of others, and that light reveals to us who we ourselves are. *Mike Mason*

■

Two are better than one,
because they have a good return for their work:
If one falls down, his friend can help him up.
But pity the man who falls and has no one to help him up!
Ecclesiastes 4:9-10

■

People with deep and lasting friendships may be introverts, extroverts, young, old, dull, intelligent, homely, good-looking; but the one characteristic they always have in common is openness. They have a certain transparency, allowing people to see what is in their hearts. *Alan Loy McGinnis,* The Friendship Factor

■

When you help someone else up the hill, you reach the top yourself. *Anonymous*

■

It is no small thing to be on terms of friendship with God. *Mrs. Charles E. Cowman,* Streams in the Desert

■

The door to the human heart can be opened only from the inside. *Jo Petty,* Apples of Gold

■

Real friends are those who, when you've made a fool of
yourself, don't feel that you've done a permanent job.
Anonymous

■

What a Friend we have in Jesus, all our sins and griefs
to bear.
What a privilege to carry everything to God in prayer.
Joseph Scriven, "What a Friend We Have in Jesus"

■

There is a friend who sticks closer than a brother.
Proverbs 18:24

■

Friendship is to be purchased only by friendship.
Unknown

■

The best way to form a friendship is to become interested
in other people, not by trying to interest people in you.
Dale Carnegie

■

The only way to have a friend is to be one.   *Unknown*

■

Here's to the friends that I love best,
    To those who have always stood the test;
To the friends I love who are tried and true,
    Friends that are old, and those that are new.

Life at its best to most is a trial,
   'Tis friendship that makes life really worthwhile.
E.K. Orr

■

A real friend is a person who walks in when everybody
else walks out.   *Unknown*

■

A person is the single most limitless entity in creation,
and if there is anything that is even more unlimited and
unrestrained in its possibilities than is a person, then it is
two people together.   *Mike Mason*

■

CHOOSE

The single clenched fist lifted and ready,
Or the open asking hand held out and waiting.
Choose:
For we meet by one or the other.   *Carl Sandburg*

■

Our restlessness within can only be met by the revelation of
God's eternal friendship and love for us.   *Margaret Bottome*

■

In each one of us the holiest and neediest and most sensi-
tive place of all has been made and is reserved for God
alone, so that only He can enter there. No one else can
love us as He does, and no one else can be the sort of
Friend to us that He is.   *Mike Mason*

53

■

No man has penned a truer line since the old world knew
  birth—
I wouldn't trade a friend of mine for all the gold on earth.
Luke McLuke

■

May the hinges of friendship never grow rusty.   *Unknown*

■

How seldom we weigh our neighbor in the same balance
with ourselves.   *Thomas à Kempis*

■

Friendship is the only cement that will ever hold the
world together.   *Jo Petty,* Apples of Gold

■

A friend is a present you give yourself.   *Robert Louis
Stevenson*

■

FRIENDSHIP

I've discovered a way to stay friends forever—
There's really nothing to it.
I simply tell you what to do
And you do it!   *Shel Silverstein,* A Light in the Attic

■

O Lord, in sorrow and in joy, open thou our lives to one
another that we may live. Open thou our lives to thee that

even in dying we may never die.   *Frederick Buechner,* The
Hungering Dark

■

To get the full value of a joy, you must have somebody to
divide it with.   *Mark Twain*

■

We're not primarily put on this earth to see through one
another, but to see one another through.   *Peter DeVries,* Let
Me Count the Ways

■

Intimacy, then, is always difficult, and when it stops being
difficult it stops being intimacy.   *Andrew Greeley*

■

Becoming an expert at friendship will be one of the most
rewarding projects of your lifetime.   *Alan Loy McGinnis,* The
Friendship Factor

■

Some of the greatest men I have had the privilege of
knowing not only are the most humble, but are those who
express their humility by becoming actual servants in
their relationships with others.   *Mark O. Hatfield*

■

Greater love has no one than this, that he lay down his life
for his friends.   *John 15:13*

■

To be is to be vulnerable.   *Norman O. Brown*

Money can't buy friends but you get a better class of enemies. *Spike Milligan*

■

Every life we touch is a field, everything we do and all the words we speak, are seed. What will the harvest be? *Rowland*

■

The only way to get the best of an argument is to avoid it. *Dale Carnegie*

■

We gain nothing by being with such as ourselves: we encourage each other in mediocrity. I am always longing to be with men more excellent than myself. *Charles Lamb*

■

Do unto others as if you were the others. *Elbert Hubbard*

■

If you approach each new person you meet in the spirit of adventure, you will find yourself endlessly fascinated by the new channels of thought and experience and personality that you encounter. *Eleanor Roosevelt*

■

As iron sharpens iron,
so one man sharpens another.
Proverbs 27:17

■

Make new friends, but keep the old—
One is silver, and the other gold.
Children's song

■

A loyal friend laughs at your jokes when they're not so
good, and sympathizes with your problems when they're
not so bad. *Arnold H. Glasow*

■

If a man be gracious to strangers, it shows that he is a
citizen of the world, and his heart is no island, cut off
from other islands, but a continent that joins them both.
Francis Bacon

■

A friend loves at all times. *Proverbs 17:17*

■

There is no such thing as life apart from relationship . . .
no life apart from the sharing of ourselves with another.
Mike Mason

■ ■ ■ ■ ■ ■ ■ ■ ■ ■ ■ ■ ■ ■ ■

LOOKING FOR LOVE

In a world where people fall in and out of love as often as
they go to the movies, look for the source of real love.
Get ready to love by learning to love God, who is Love itself.

The first duty of love is to listen. *Paul Tillich*

■

My heart is a bargain today. Will you take it? *W.C. Fields*

■

Respect is love in plain clothes. *Frankie Byrne*

■

The supreme happiness of life is the conviction of being
loved for yourself, or, more correctly, being loved in spite
of yourself. *Victor Hugo*

■

Love at first sight is a great time-saver. *Unknown*

■

Love must be learned, and learned again and again; there
is no end to it. Hate needs no instruction, but wants only
to be provoked. *Katherine Anne Porter*

■

Love is a feeling to be learned. *Walter Trobisch*

■

f music be the food of love, play on. *William Shakespeare, Twelfth Night*

■

'Tis better to have loved and lost than never to have loved at all. *Alfred Lord Tennyson*

■

'Tis better to have loved and lost—than just to have lost! *C. Stephen Board*

■

True love is a gift on which no return is demanded. To love unselfishly is its own reward. To love for fulfillment, satisfaction, or pride is no love. *Og Mandino*

■

Love asks for everything. Not just for a little bit, or a whole lot, but for everything. And unless one is challenged to give everything, one is not really in love.
Mike Mason, The Mystery of Marriage

■

But God demonstrates his own love for us in this: While we were still sinners, Christ died for us. *Romans 5:8*

■

Love cannot be wasted. It makes no difference where it is bestowed, it always brings in big returns. *Unknown*

■

The arc of love from God to men
     orbiting, goes to him again.
My love, to loving God above,
     captures *me* in the round of love.
Luci Shaw, "Circles," Listen to the Green

■

Love one another. As I have loved you, so you must love one another. *John 13:34*

■

Love without ceasing,
     Give without measure—
Who can exhaust
     God's limitless treasure?
Malcolm Schloss

■

To love at all is to be vulnerable. Love anything, and your heart will certainly be wrung and possibly broken. . . . The only place outside Heaven where you can be perfectly safe from all the dangers and perturbations of love is Hell. *C.S. Lewis*, The Four Loves

■

True love is not a feeling by which we are overwhelmed. It is a committed, thoughtful decision.   *M. Scott Peck*, The Road Less Traveled

■

The capacity to care is the thing which gives life its deepest significance.   *Pablo Casals*

■

unless you love someone nothing else makes any sense. *e.e. cummings*

■

It is a long and hard road; it is an altar of sacrifice. . . . Love is the only way to our human destiny and to the feet of God, who is love.   *John Powell*, Why Am I Afraid to Love?

■

The most prevalent failure of Christian love is the failure to express it.   *Rev. Paul E. Johnson*, Christian Love

■

Love consists in this, that two solitudes protect and touch and greet each other.   *Rainer Maria Rilke*

■

Love must be tough.   *James Dobson*

■

Love is the medicine for the sickness of mankind. We can live if we have love.   *Karl Menninger*

■

Love is like quicksilver in the hand. Leave the fingers open and it stays. Clutch it, and it darts away.   *Dorothy Parker*

■

I like not only to be loved, but also to be told that I am loved.   *George Eliot*

■

To love, and be loved, is the greatest happiness of existence.   *Sydney Smith*

■

Adam invented love at first sight, one of the greatest labor saving devices the world ever saw.   *Josh Billings*

■

The risk of love
is that of being unreturned.
Luci Shaw, "Perfect love banishes fear,"   Listen to the Green

■

Love your enemy—it'll drive him nuts.   *Unknown*

■

Love brings people out into the light. . . . Love aims at revelation, at a clarifying and defining of our true natures. It is a sort of sharpening process, a paring away of dull and lifeless exteriors so that the keen new edge of a person's new self can begin to flash and gleam in the light of day. *Mike Mason,* The Mystery of Marriage

■

Love never fails. *1 Corinthians 13:8*

■

Love is never afraid of giving too much. *Unknown*

■

If we empty our hearts of self, God will fill them with his love. *Charles H. Spurgeon*

■ ■ ■ ■ ■ ■ ■ ■ ■ ■ ■ ■ ■ ■ ■

BUILDING CHARACTER

Graduation is a time of change, and all change points are crucial times for setting personal goals and establishing personal habits. Give some time and attention to the way you are "working out" and "shaping up" on the inside.

Everybody thinks of changing humanity, and nobody thinks of changing himself. *Leo Tolstoy*

■

Happiness is not the end of life: character is. *Henry Ward Beecher, "Life Thoughts"*

■

Reputation is what men and women think of us. Character is what God and angels know of us. *Thomas Paine*

■

A good name is more desirable than great riches; to be esteemed is better than silver or gold. *Proverbs 22:1*

■

You are redeemed to be set aside for God's special use and made a partaker of his moral perfection. *John White,* The Fight

■

Make it your ambition to lead a quiet life, to mind your own business and to work with your hands, just as we told

you, so that your daily life may win the respect of out-
siders and so that you will not be dependent on anybody.
1 Thessalonians 4:11-12

■

The joy of heaven begins as soon as we attain the character of heaven.   *Keith L. Brooks,* The Cream Book: Sentence
Sermons

■

Character is like the foundation to a house . . . it is below
the surface.   *Unknown*

■

Self-discipline is usually love, translated into action.
M. Scott Peck, The Road Less Traveled

■

Initiative is doing the right thing without being told.
Elbert Hubbard

■

The highest reward for a man's toil is not what he gets
for it, but rather what he becomes by it.   *Jo Petty,* Apples
of Gold

■

Christian character is not an inheritance; each individual
must build it for himself.   *Unknown*

■

A moment's insight is sometimes worth a life's experience.   *Oliver W. Holmes*

Greatness is a two-faced coin—and its reverse is humility.
Unknown

■

If I take care of my character, my reputation will take care
of itself.   *Dwight L. Moody*

■

A good name keeps its lustre in the dark.   *John Ray*

■

Let love and faithfulness never leave you;
bind them around your neck,
write them on the tablet of your heart.
Then you will win favor and a good name
in the sight of God and man.
Proverbs 3:3-4

■

I look upon the sublime and childish virtues of veracity
and honesty as the root of all that is sublime in character.
Ralph Waldo Emerson

■

Be at war with your vices, at peace with your neighbors,
and let every new year find you a better man.   *Benjamin
Franklin*

■

Occasions do not make a man either strong or weak, but
they show what he is.   *Thomas à Kempis*

■

Character is like a tree and reputation like its shadow. The shadow is what we think of it; the tree is the real thing.
Abraham Lincoln

■

Character is best formed in the stormy billows of the world. *Goethe*

■

I hope I shall possess firmness and virtue enough to maintain what I consider the most enviable of all titles, that of an "honest man." *George Washington*

■

Sometimes when I get up in the morning . . . I feel like I've just got to bite a cat! I feel like if I don't bite a cat before sundown, I'll go crazy! But then I just take a deep breath and forget about it. That's what's known as real maturity. *Snoopy (Peanuts)*

■

God's preparing His heroes; and when opportunity comes, He can fit them into their place in a moment, and the world will wonder where they came from. *A.B. Simpson*

■

Holiness is not only expected, it is the promised birthright of every Christian. . . . To be holy is to be morally blameless. It is to be separated from sin and, therefore, consecrated to God. *Jerry Bridges,* The Pursuit of Holiness

■

The man who masters himself is free. *Epictetus*

■

He who reigns within himself, and rules passions, desires, and fears, is more than a king. *John Milton*

■

Character is much easier kept than recovered. *Thomas Paine*

■

Character is what you are in the dark. *Dwight L. Moody*

■

Character in matters great and small consists in a man steadily pursuing the things of which he feels himself capable. *Unknown*

■

The only reputation that matters is your reputation in heaven. *Keith L. Brooks,* The Cream Book: Sentence Sermons

■

The measure of a man's real character is what he would do if he knew he would never be found out. *Thomas Macauley*

■

Dwell in the life and love and power and wisdom of God, in unity one with another and with God; and the peace and wisdom of God fill your hearts, that nothing may rule in you but the life, which stands in the Lord God. *George Fox*

■

Our acts make or mar us—we are the children of our own deeds. *Victor Hugo*

■

Try not to become a man of success, but rather try to become a man of value. *Albert Einstein*

■

Make yourself an honest man and then you may be sure there is one less rascal in the world. *Thomas Carlyle*

■

A peace above all earthly dignities, a still and quiet conscience. *William Shakespeare*

■

He has showed you, O man, what is good. And what does the LORD require of you? To act justly and to love mercy and to walk humbly with your God. *Micah 6:8*

■

No man doth safely rule but he that hath learned gladly to obey. *Thomas à Kempis,* The Imitation of Christ

■

When our vision of God is one of a God of relentless tenderness, we ultimately become tender ourselves.
Brennan Manning

■

Humility is to make a right estimate of oneself. *Charles H. Spurgeon*

■

It is not by a man's purse, but by his character, that he is rich or poor. *Robert Louis Stevenson*

■

Fear God and keep his commandments,
for this is the whole duty of man.
Ecclesiastes 12:13

■

Character is what God knows you are. *Unknown*

■

No legacy is so rich as honesty. *William Shakespeare*

■

It is not by a man's purse, but by his character, that he is
rich or poor. *Robert Louis Stevenson*

■

Blessed are the pure in heart, for they will see God.
Matthew 5:8

■

There's no heavier burden than great potential. *Linus
(Peanuts)*

■

To go on being filled with the Spirit is to grow in holiness
continually. *John White,* The Fight

■

To thine own self be true. *William Shakespeare*

■

Modesty is the art of encouraging people to find out for
themselves how wonderful you are. *Unknown*

71

You better not compromise yourself. It's all you got.
Janis Joplin

■

Integrity means an uncompromising adherence to a code of moral values: utter sincerity, honesty, and candor. It is an absence of deception, expediency, artificiality, or shallowness of any kind.   *John Souter*

■

Self-discipline is when your conscience tells you to do something and you don't talk back.   *W.K. Hope*

■

Joy is found in obedience.   *Richard Foster,* The Celebration of Discipline

■

Maturity is the capacity to endure uncertainty.   *John Finley*

■

Bad habits are like a comfortable bed—easy to get into, but hard to get out of.   *Unknown*

■

A Christian is a person who makes you think of Jesus.
Robert C. Savage, Pocket Quips

■

True repentance empties the soul of sin, separates the self from sin, and sets us free to follow God, to live rightly,

wholesomely, as we were meant to live.   *David Augsburger,*
The Freedom of Forgiveness

·

The person who has the approval of his own conscience
has a powerful ally.   *Unknown*

·

When the fight begins within himself, a man's worth
something.   *Robert Browning*

·

He who most clearly discerns the perfect character of
Jesus will be most urgent in prayer for grace to be like
him.   *Charles H. Spurgeon*

·

Talent is nurtured in solitude; character is formed in the
stormy billows of the world.   *Goethe*

·

A good name is better than fine perfume.   *Ecclesiastes 7:1*

· · · · · · · · · · · ·

GREAT EXPECTATIONS

The future stretches out before you, like a white canvas
ready to be painted with the bright colors of your life.
Don't fear the days to come, but look forward in faith and
anticipate the blessings God has for you right around the corner.

The future is as bright as the promises of God. We know
not what the future holds, but we know who holds the
future.   *Robert C. Savage,* Pocket Quips

■

Here's to your future,
   Your present and your past.
May each new day
   Be happier than the last.
Unknown

■

The future is a convenient place for dreams.   *Anatole France*

■

For the Son of Man is going to come in his Father's glory
with his angels, and then he will reward each person ac-
cording to what he has done.   *Matthew 16:27*

■

Let yesterday trouble you unduly today and you will ruin
tomorrow.   *Unknown*

■

Hitch your wagon to a star. *Ralph Waldo Emerson*

■

The future's so bright I gotta wear shades! *Snoopy (Peanuts)*

■

God is down in front. He is in the tomorrows. It is tomorrow that fills men with dread. God is there already. *F.B. Meyer*

■

Where will I be five years from now? I delight in not knowing. That's one of the greatest things about life—its wonderful surprises. *Marlo Thomas*

■

Our Lord holds His most vital and best things in store for those who mean business, for those who hunger and thirst for His very best. *Miles J. Stanford,* Principles of Spiritual Growth

·

I am willing to go anywhere provided it be forward.
David Livingstone

·

Soon He's coming back to welcome me
Far beyond the starry sky;
I shall wing my flight to worlds unknown,
I shall reign with Him on high.
Luther Bridgers, "There's Within My Heart a Melody"

·

I've developed a new philosophy. . . . I only dread one
day at a time.   *Charlie Brown (Peanuts)*

·

We are to live but one day at a time, but we are living for
eternity in that one day.   *Unknown*

·

The present moment more resembles eternity than any
other, because in it the present, the past, and the future
converge.   *Eugene Peterson,* Traveling Light

·

The future is something you shouldn't worry about because
it may not last long.   *Evan Esar,* Esar's Comic Dictionary

·

Get excited about your home in heaven with God—it will
change the way you live each day here on earth while you

wait for the day you'll be home forever.   *Annette Heinrich,*
One in a Zillion

Aim at heaven and you will get earth thrown in. Aim at earth
and you will get neither.   *C.S. Lewis,* Mere Christianity

The same everlasting Father who cares for you today
will take care of you tomorrow, and every day.   *Frances
de Sales*

■

The future is that period of time in which our affairs
prosper, our friends are true, and our happiness is assured.
Ambrose Bierce

■

The point of living, and of being an optimist, is to be
foolish enough to believe the best is yet to come.   *Peter
Ustinov*

■

When Christ shall come with shout of acclamation,
and take me home, what joy shall fill my heart.
Then I shall bow in humble adoration,
And there proclaim, "My God, how great Thou art!"
Stuart K. Hine, "How Great Thou Art"

■

Fogetting what is behind and straining toward what is
ahead, I press on toward the goal to win the prize for
which God has called me heavenward in Christ Jesus.
Philippians 3:13-14

■

The only limit to our realization of tomorrow will be our
doubts of today.
Franklin D. Roosevelt

Listen, I tell you a mystery: We will not all sleep, but we will all be changed—in a flash, in the twinkling of an eye, at the last trumpet. For the trumpet will sound, the dead will be raised imperishable, and we will be changed.
1 Corinthians 15:51-52

You can't start worrying about what's going to happen. You get spastic enough worrying about what's happening now. *Lauren Bacall*

You better live your best and act your best and think your best today; for today is the sure preparation for tomorrow and all the other tomorrows that follow.
Harriet Martineau

Whatever the Lord takes in hand He will accomplish; hence past mercies are guarantees for the future and admirable reasons for continuing to cry unto Him. *Charles H. Spurgeon*

The pace of events is moving so fast that unless we can find some way to keep our sights on tomorrow, we cannot expect to be in touch with today. *Dean Rusk*

What lies behind us and what lies before us are tiny matters compared to what lies within us. *Ralph Waldo Emerson*

My interest is in the future because I am going to spend the rest of my life there.
Charles F. Kettering

■

Perhaps the best thing about the future is that it only comes one day at a time.
Dean Acheson

■

Life is the only sentence that doesn't end with a period.
Louis Gould

■

Life with Christ is an endless hope; without him a hopeless end. *Merv Rosell,* Driftwood

■

I never think of the future—it comes soon enough. *Albert Einstein*

■

We must see to it that enthusiasm for the future does not give rise to contempt for the past. *Pope Paul VI*

■

He who provides for this life, but takes no care for eternity, is wise for a moment, but a fool forever.
Tillotson

■

In my Father's house are many rooms; if it were not so, I would have told you. I am going there to prepare a place for you. And if I go and prepare a place for you, I will come back and take you to be with me that you also may be where I am. *John 14:2-3*

■ ■ ■ ■ ■ ■ ■ ■ ■ ■ ■ ■ ■ ■ ■

INDEX

à Kempis, Thomas, *54, 66, 70*
Acheson, Dean, *80*
action, *8, 10, 23, 37-38, 65*
Addison, Joseph, *25*
adventure, *1, 11, 56*
affection, *30*
ambition, *64*
Amiel, Henri, *44*
Armerding, Hudson T., *34*
Augsburger, David, *73*
Augustine, *19*
Aurelius, Marcus, *45*
Avebury, Lord, *16*

Bacall, Lauren, *79*
Bach, T.J., *7*
Bacon, Francis, *57*
Baldwin, James, *31*
Barclay, William, *11*
Barth, Karl, *49*
beauty, *25, 30*
Beecher, Henry Ward, *4, 6,
    17, 64*
beginning, *1, 11, 20, 30*
Bevan, Ancurin, *17*
Bierce, Ambrose, *78*

Billings, Josh, *40, 62*
Blake, William, *23, 46*
blessing, *9, 20, 23, 34*
Board, C. Stephen, *59*
boast, *5*
Bonhoeffer, Deitrich, *38*
Borge, Victor, *40*
Bottome, Margaret, *53*
Bridgers, Luther, *76*
Bridges, Jerry, *67*
Brooks, Keith L., *3, 7, 31,
    65, 69*
Brooks, Phillips, *21*
Brown, Norman O., *55*
Browning, Robert, *28, 73*
Bruner, Margaret E., *36*
Buechner, Frederick, *13, 55*
burden, *71*
Burgess, Gelett, *43*
Burke, Edmund, *35*
Butler, Samuel, *50*
Byrne, Frankie, *58*

Carey, William, *31*
Carlyle, Thomas, *28, 48, 70*
Carnegie, Dale, *28, 52, 56*

Casals, Pablo, *61*

Chambers, Oswald, *50*

change, *9-10, 64, 76*

character, *45, 64-67, 69-71, 73*

Chesterton, G.K., *10, 19, 29*

choice, *13, 15, 17*

college, *8*

Colson, Charles, *3*

compromise, *72*

confidence, *20, 23, 47*

conscience, *24, 70, 72-73*

Coolidge, Calvin, *38*

Cosby, Bill, *17*

courage, *18, 28*

Cowman, Mrs. Charles E., *10, 51*

crossroads, *9-10*

Crowe, John H., *47*

cummings, e.e., 61

David, Donald K., *1*

decision, *14, 16, 18, 61*

deeds, *23, 29, 33, 69*

De Mille, Agnes, *16*

dependence, *20*

de Sales, Frances, *78*

destination, *12*

destiny, *13, 61*

DeVries, Peter, *55*

Dickinson, Emily, *37, 47*

direction, *3, 9*

discipline, *1, 72*

Dobson, James, *62*

doubt, *16, 20, 22-23*

dreams, *1, 74*

duty, *36, 48, 58, 71*

Eavey, C.B., *9, 14, 18, 22, 41*

Eddy, Sherwood, *19*

Edison, Thomas, *2*

Edman, V. Raymond, *37*

education, *1-2, 4, 6-7, 10*

Einstein, Albert, *70, 80*

Eliot, George, *15, 62*

Eliot, T.S., *22, 25*

Eller, Vernard, *49*

Emerson, Ralph Waldo, *30, 36, 38, 66, 75, 79*

Epictetus, *68*

Esar, Evan, *1, 6, 9, 76*

essentials, *25*

eternity, *25, 45-46, 76, 80*

evil, *14, 18*

excellence, *1*

expectation, *20-21*

experience, *56, 65*

84

Faber, F.W., *29*
failure, *17, 61*
faith, *6, 10, 19, 20-23, 37, 74*
faithfulness, *3, 66*
Faunce, *11*
fellowship, *18*
Fields, W.C., *58*
Finley, John, *72*
Forsyth, P.T., *38*
forward, *74, 76*
Foster, Richard, *72*
foundation, *19, 29, 65*
Fox, George, *69*
France, Anatole, *33, 74*
Franklin, Benjamin, *27, 31, 35, 66, 78*
Fremantle, Anne, *42*
friend, *2, 9, 50-54, 57*
friendship, *51-55*
Friesen, Garry, *16*
Frost, Robert, *2, 9*
Fuller, Thomas, *4, 42*
future, *27, 74-76, 78-80*

Garfield, James A., *7*
generous, *4, 29*
genius, *2*
Glasow, Arnold H., *2, 57*
Gleason, Gene, *8*

goal, *24, 78*
God, *3, 6-7, 11-29, 31, 34, 44, 49-52, 54, 58, 60-61, 63-64, 66-67, 69-72, 74-75, 78*
God-dependence, *20*
God's Word, *3, 20, 23*
Goethe, *37, 45, 67, 73*
Gould, Louis, *80*
graduation, *7, 9, 64*
Graham, Billy, *18*
great, *6-7, 14, 18, 29, 31, 33, 37, 58, 64, 69, 71, 78*
Greeley, Andrew, *55*
grief, *42*
Grimes, Martha, *1*
growth, *7, 9, 15, 75*
guide, *12*
guidelines, *3*

happiness, *11, 18, 25, 43, 45, 58, 62, 64, 78*
Hatfield, Mark O., *55*
Havens, Paul Swain, *8*
heart, *18, 20-21, 42-43, 46-49, 51, 57-58, 61, 66, 71, 76, 78*
heaven, *50, 61, 65, 69, 76-77*
Heinrich, Annette, *77*

help, *37, 51*
Helps, Arthur, *5*
Hemingway, Ernest, *28*
Herbert, George, *27, 42*
Hill, Napoleon, *10*
Hine, Stuart K., *78*
holiness, *14, 37, 67, 71*
Holmes, Oliver W., *65*
Holy Spirit, *3*
honesty, *66, 71, 72*
hope, *19, 21, 25, 28-29, 36,*
   49, 67, 72, 80
Hope, W.K., *72*
Horace, *1*
Hubbard, Elbert, *15, 18, 30,*
   56, 65
Hughes, Kent and Barbara,
   3
Hugo, Victor, *58, 69*
humor, *40, 42, 48*
Huntington, F.D., *37*
Hutchins, Robert, *1*

ideals, *12*
ignorance, *2, 6*
individual, *18, 65*
initiative, *23, 65*
inspiration, *2*
integrity, *72*

intelligence, *8*
Irving, Washington, *14*

Jefferson, Thomas, *31*
Jerome, Father, O.S.B., *44*
Johnson, Kenneth, *2*
Johnson, Paul E., *61*
Joplin, Janis, *72*
joy, *10, 20, 40, 46-47, 49,*
   54-55, 65, 72, 78

Keller, Helen, *26, 33*
Kettering, Charles F., *80*
Kiemel, Ann, *36*
kindness, *34, 39*
Kissinger, Henry, *15*
Kleiser, Grenville, *42*
Knebel, Fletcher, *14*
knowledge, *2-4, 6-7, 10, 34*

Lamb, Charles, *56*
laugh, *30, 41-42, 44, 46, 48*
laughter, *40-41, 43, 45, 48*
learning, *2, 6, 8, 58*
Lee, William, *11*
Leterman, Elmer, *35*
Lewis, C.S., *11, 19, 25, 50,*
   61, 77
liberty, *16*

light, *4, 25, 32, 37, 51, 54, 63, 76*
Lincoln, Abraham, *39, 44, 67*
Lindbergh, Anne Morrow, *29*
living, *4, 16, 27-30, 76, 78*
Livingstone, David, *76*
Longfellow, Henry Wadsworth, *38*
Lowell, J.R., *18*
Lucado, Max, *37*
Luther, Martin, *28, 34, 76*
Lyon, Mary, *34*

Macauley, Thomas, *69*
MacDonald, George, *12, 16*
Mandino, Og, *59*
Manning, Brennan, *70*
Markham, Edwin, *13*
Marshall, Peter, *33*
Martineau, Harriet, *79*
Mason, Mike, *51, 53-54, 57, 60, 63*
maturity, *67, 72*
McConkey, James, *20*
McGinnis, Alan Loy, *55*
McLuke, Luke, *54*
Meir, Golda, *42*
Menninger, Karl, *62*
Meyer, F.B., *11, 75*

Milligan, Spike, *56*
Milton, John, *33, 68*
Ming, Wang, *8*
mistake, *15, 44*
modesty, *71*
Mohammed, *34*
Montaigne, Michael, *44*
Moody, Dwight L., *28, 66, 69*
Morris, Lloyd, *43*
Mottmann, Jurgen, *44*
Müller, George, *20-21, 25*
Murray, Andrew, *21*

Nabokov, Vladimir, *5*
Nash, Ogden, *48*
neighbor, *54*
Newton, Joseph Fort, *30*
Newton, Sir Isaac, *2*
noble, *45*
nonsense, *8, 40, 44*

obedience, *3, 72*
Ogilvie, Lloyd John, *33*
opportunity, *30, 34, 67*
Orr, E.K., *53*
Oxenham, John, *16*

Paine, Thomas, *64, 69*
Palmer, Kenyon, *29*

Parker, Dorothy, *40*, *62*
past, *74*, *76*, *79-80*
path, *10*, *12*
patience, *15*
peace, *66*, *69-70*
Peck, M. Scott, *61*, *65*
Pedersen, Eldon, *8*
Penn, William, *37*
Peterson, Eugene, *76*
Petty, Jo, 2, *21*, *27*, *30*, *51*, *54*, *65*
philosophy, *76*
Plato, *4*
play, *59*
Poole, Mary Pettibone, *41*
Pope Paul VI, *80*
Porter, David, *15*
Porter, Katherine Anne, *58*
potential, *25*, *71*
Pound, Ezra, *28*
Powell, A., *7*
Powell, John, *61*
power, *16*, *33*, *38*, *43*, *49*, *69*
praise, *3*
prayer, *52*, *73*
preparation, *1*, *8*, *79*
pride, *59*
Prochnow, Herbert V., *27*
profession, *1*

promises, *19*, *22*, *74*

questions, 2-3, *13*

Ray, John, *66*
Reichel, *35*
relationship, *7*, *15*, *57*
religion, *11*, *26*, *33*
reputation, *64*, *66-67*, *69*
respect, *30*, *58*, *65*
responsibility, *38*
Richter, John Paul, *4*
Rilke, Rainer Maria, *61*
road, *9*, *12*, *17*, *29*, *61*, *65*
Roger Rabbit, *46*
Roosevelt, Eleanor, *56*
Roosevelt, Franklin D., *78*
Roosevelt, Theodore, *38*
Rosell, Merv, *19*, *47*, *80*
Rowland, *56*
Rusk, Dean, *79*
Russell, Bertrand, *15*

salvation, *6*, *19*, *21*
Sandburg, Carl, *54*
satisfaction, *34*, *59*
Savage, Robert C., *6*, *20*, *22-23*, *33*, *42*, *72*, *74*
Schimmels, Cliff, *5*

88

Schloss, Malcolm, *60*

Schultz, Charles M., *43*

Schurz, Carl, *12*

Schweitzer, Albert, *31, 35*

Scriven, Joseph, *52*

self, *2, 20, 30, 63, 65, 71-72*

self-confidence, *2*

self-dependence, *20*

self-discipline, *65, 72*

Seneca, *4, 34*

serve, *14, 24, 33, 39, 47*

service, *31, 34-35, 38*

Shakespeare, William, *49, 59, 70-71*

Shannon, Dan C., *2*

Shaw, George Bernard, *27, 43*

Shaw, Luci, *10, 60, 62*

Shedd, Charles, *35*

Sheldon, Charles, *13*

Silverstein, Shel, *32, 54*

Simpson, A.B., *67*

smile, *41-42, 45-47*

Smith, Sydney, *62*

society, *2*

solitude, *2, 73*

Souter, John, *72*

Spurgeon, Charles H., *21, 63, 70, 73, 79*

Stanford, Miles J., *75*

Stead, Louisa M.R., *23*

Stevenson, Robert Louis, *44, 48, 70-71*

Stoney, J.B., *20*

strength, *12, 18, 21, 33*

struggle, *4*

study, *1, 3*

success, *1, 3, 5-8, 17, 70*

talent, *73*

temper, *2*

Tennyson, Alfred Lord, *7, 59*

Thomas, Marlo, *75*

Thorold, A.W., *20*

Thurber, James, *40*

Tillich, Paul, *20, 58*

Tillotson, *80*

today, *28, 31, 58, 74, 78-79*

Tolstoy, Leo, *64*

tomorrow, *31, 74-75, 78-79*

travel, *12*

Travers, P.L., *48*

Trobisch, Walter, *58*

trust, *11, 13, 19-21, 23, 34*

truth, *9, 18, 40*

Tucker, Jeff and Ramona, *26*

Turner, Steve, *11*

Twain, Mark, *41, 55*

uncertainty, *2, 15, 72*
Ustinov, Peter, *78*

Van Dyke, Henry, *12, 39*
vision, *30, 43, 70*

Ward, William Arthur, *4, 6,
    9, 17, 64*
Washington, George, *14, 67*
Waterman, Nixon, *47*
Wells, M.P., *42*
Wesley, Susanna, *24*
White, John, *15, 18, 21, 23,
    64, 71*
Whitehead, Alfred North, *1*
Wilcox, Ella Wheeler, *41, 45*
Wilde, Oscar, *4*
Wilkinson, Kate B., *24*

Winters, Carl S., *50*
Winters, Jonathan, *3*
wisdom, *4-5, 7-8, 30, 34, 69*
wishes, *4, 14*
wit, *40*
wonder, *11, 37, 43, 67*
Wordsworth, William, *31*
work, *4, 6-7, 23-24, 30,
    37-38, 51, 64*
world, *10, 24, 28, 30-31,
    33-34, 37, 41, 43-44, 54,
    57-58, 62, 67, 70, 73*
worry, *22, 76*
Wright, J.F., *26*

yesterday, *74*

zeal, *38*